Seashore

Lynn Huggins-Cooper

Illustrated by
Shelagh McNicholas and David Burroughs

W
FRANKLIN WATTS
LONDON•SYDNEY

About the author
Lynn Huggins-Cooper is a
lecturer in primary science
at Newcastle University and
specialises in interactive
teaching methods. She also
creates wildlife gardens for
schools and runs a
conservation club.

This edition 2008
Published by Franklin Watts
338 Euston Road, London NW1 3BH

Franklin Watts Australia
Level 17/207 Kent Street, Sydney NSW 2000

Series editor: Rachel Cooke
Art director: Jonathan Hair
Design: James Marks

A CIP catalogue record for this book is available
from the British Library.

ISBN 978 0 7496 7868 5
Printed in China

Franklin Watts is a division of Hachette Children's
Books, an Hachette Livre UK company.

Contents

David loves the seashore. Come and explore it with him.

At low **tide**, the sea is far out and the beach is huge.

When the tide turns, the water rises up the sand. At high tide, the beach is completely covered.

On the beach

David is spending the day at the beach. It is low tide, so there is lots of sand – and lots of rock pools to explore!

The tide rises and falls twice each day. The times of high tide and low tide change a little each time.

Seaweed is a plant that grows in salty seawater. There are many different kinds.

Bladderwrack has floats full of jelly and air.

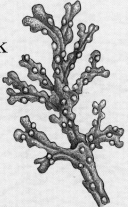

Huge kelp 'forests' grow in deeper water. They are home to lots of fish and other creatures.

Sea lettuce is bright green. It grows in shallow water near the shore.

David can smell the salty seaweed on the rocks.

David and Grandma are busy digging in the sand. There are some birds digging, too.

Look David, there are some sandpipers.

Seashore birds such as sandpipers dig about in the sand to find small creatures to eat.

Lots of creatures live in the sand. Here are some:

Cockle

Sand dollar

Lugworm

Razor shell

Why do you think a sandpiper's beak is long and pointed?

David sees some piles of sand spaghetti! And what are those strange tubes sticking out of the sand?

The piles of sand spaghetti are worm-casts made by lugworms pushing through the sand.

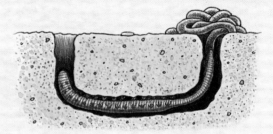

The sandy tubes are built by sand worms.

Underwater, the worm comes out of its tube and waves its **tentacles** about to catch food.

Sand contains lots of tiny pieces of broken shells and rock.

When the tide goes out, lots of things are left on the beach. These are some natural things:

Seaweed

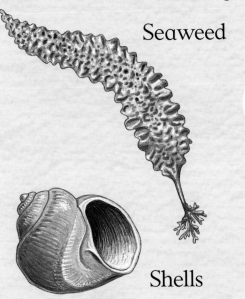

Shells

Crabs

Mermaid's purse

A mermaid's purse once held the eggs of a dog fish.

Left by the tide

David wants to decorate his sandcastle. He walks along the beach with his mum and dad to see what he can find.

Careful of that rubbish! It's horrible - and dangerous.

Rubbish can hurt sea creatures. Fishing line can tangle around the legs of sea birds.

The tide can leave rubbish behind, too.

These things are not natural, but **artificial**: they have been made by people - and thrown away by them.

Plastic bottles and bags

Old nylon rope

Fishing line

Glass

Keep an eye out for broken glass on the beach. It can cut you.

11

Most shells we find were left behind when the small animals that lived inside them died.

Some shells are made up of one part:

Egg cowrie

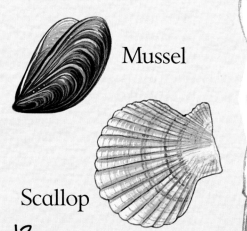

Tower shell

Other shells have two parts that open and close:

Mussel

Scallop

David shows Grandma his beach finds. She picks up a shell – and a hermit crab gives her a surprise!

Hermit crabs have no shell of their own. They find empty shells to live inside.

These are the different stages of a crab's life - its **life cycle**.

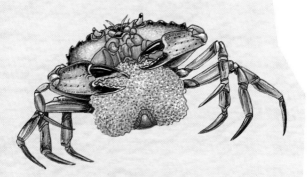

1. A female crab carries her eggs in a special flap under her belly.

David found lots of crab shells of all different sizes. Dad told him crabs grow out of the shells and leave them behind.

2. When they hatch, the babies do not look like their parents!

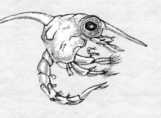

3. Eventually, the crab looks like its parents - but tiny!

4. As the crab grows bigger, it sheds its old shell - for us to find on the beach!

13

As the tide goes down, water gets left behind and forms pools. Lots of animals live in the **rock pools**.

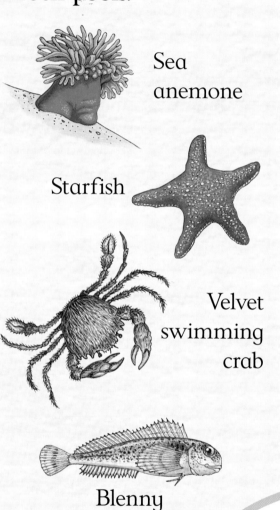

Sea anemone

Starfish

Velvet swimming crab

Blenny

Prawn

14

Rock pooling

David goes to look for more creatures in a big, weedy rock pool.

What's that red thing?

Can you find all these creatures in David's rock pool?

A sea anemone. It looks very different out of water.

Sea anemones attach themselves to rocks. They catch food in the water with their tentacles.

Out of the water they close up to make sure they don't dry out.

Be careful when exploring rock pools. Don't go too deep and ALWAYS make sure you leave before the tide comes in and covers the pools up again!

David takes his net and catches a prawn hiding in the seaweed. He has to move very fast!

Prawns eat bits of dead fish and shellfish. They move quickly and are hard to see as they are almost see-through.

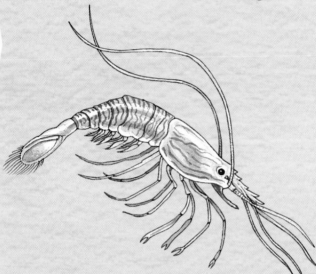

Prawns have long feelers to help them find their food in the sand and rocks.

How do you think being quick and hard to see helps the prawn?

Sometimes larger animals catch and eat them - sea birds, big fish and people.

When you see prawns at the shops, they are usually bright pink. This is because they have been cooked.

Dad puts David's prawn in a clear plastic box full of seawater. It waves its feelers at them! Then Dad carefully puts it back in the pool.

! ! !

You can catch animals in rock pools to look at them, but always handle them very carefully and put them back where you found them.

17

Among the dunes

It's time for lunch – a picnic in the grassy dunes. David makes sure everyone collects their rubbish.

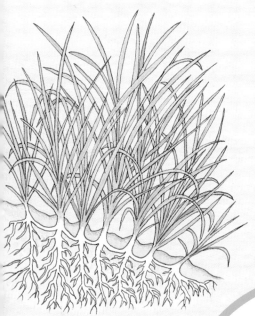

Dunes are mounds of sand that form when the sand is blown into piles by the wind coming off the sea.

The **roots** of grasses and other plants help keep the dunes together.

As well as by the sea, where else do you think you might find sand dunes?

David is glad to have a rug to sit on. There are all sorts of prickly plants around.

Are the seashore plants different to the plants in your garden, or at the park? How?

Plants that grow at the seaside have to be tough - or the salty water, wind and sun would dry them out.

Some plants have rubbery leaves:

Sea kale

Sea holly

Some plants have very thin leaves so they do not lose lots of water:

Marram grass

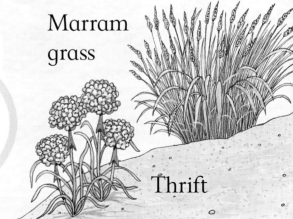

Thrift

Following the fish

David and Mum walk down to the harbour. Seagulls shriek in the air and try to steal fish from the boat coming in.

There are lots of birds to spot beside the sea.

Seagulls eat fish - and any scraps they can find. They will **scavenge** for food on rubbish tips far from the sea.

20

Cormorants dive under the water to catch fish.

Puffins catch sandeels and other fish in their big beaks.

? ? ?

Look back at page 8. How does a sandpiper use its long beak?

Oystercatchers eat shellfish. They use their long beaks to open cockles and mussels.

Turnstones eat insects. They use their beaks to tip up stones and seaweed to find sand hoppers and sea slaters.

Edible crabs can grow as big as saucers!

Lobsters have thick shells and powerful pincers.

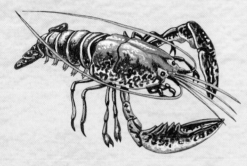

Mackerel move quickly through the water in big groups called **shoals**.

Flounders are flat fish. They glide along the ocean floor. They are hard to see!

The fisherman shows David and Mum what he has caught in the deep water far out at sea.

Why do you think flounders are hard to see?

22

The fisherman doesn't want the small green octopus. He shows it to David before he puts it back in the water.

An octopus has eight arms or tentacles which it uses to pull itself along the sea floor, and to catch its food.

It often eats crabs and lobsters.

An octopus can squeeze its soft body into holes and cracks to hide.

There are 150 different types of octopus. The smallest can fit on your hand, the largest is bigger and heavier than a man.

Pebbles and rocks

David and Mum say goodbye to the fisherman and walk back along the beach. David picks up some smooth, glistening pebbles.

This is how a pebble is made:

1. Long ago, a pebble was part of a rocky **cliff**.

2. The waves pounded the cliff and a rough, jagged rock broke off into the sea.

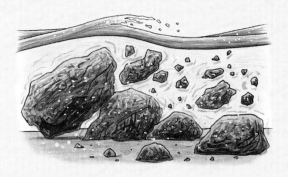

3. Under the water, the rock was bashed against other rocks and stones by the waves. It broke up into smaller pieces.

4. The waves kept tumbling the smaller rock over and over, rubbing it against sand and other stones. Any rough edges were slowly smoothed away.

5. The piece of rough rock became the smooth, small pebble we find on the beach.

David has made a real find – a fossil of an ancient sea creature.

That was alive at the time of the dinosaurs!

Fossils are the marks left by ancient animals that were buried in mud millions of years ago. Very slowly the mud became hard rock.

25

Seaside treasures

David has made a seaside museum on the sand. He will take home some of his finds and leave others to be washed away by the tide.

Here are some extra things David found. Which can you find in his seaside museum?

Driftwood smoothed by the sea

Whelk egg case

Which of David's finds can you name? Look back through the book to remind yourself.

Cuttlebone from a cuttlefish

Coral

Dry starfish

Goose barnacle

Try this yourself

Have some seashore fun –
on the beach or back at home.

Barnacle behaviour

Barnacles are rough white shells that are found on rocks by the sea. They are stuck hard and never seem to move. When covered with sea water, they look quite different!

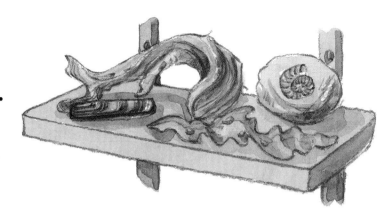

1. Find a stone covered with barnacles. Put it in a bucket full of sea water. Watch what happens.

2. Soon, the barnacles open at the top and wave feathery 'fingers' in the water, looking for tiny bits of food!

3. Afterwards, put the stone carefully back where you found it.

Show off your finds

After you've been to the beach - or any trip where you've collected things - you could make your own museum to display your finds. You could put them on a shelf or window sill and write labels.

For smaller finds, divide up a box with card to make a display case.

A rock pool display

Make a rock pool for your beach finds. If you haven't been to the beach, you can make shells and animals out of clay or Plasticine.

1. Cut a rock pool shape out of a large piece of corrugated card.

2. Crumple up newspaper into rock shapes and stick them around the card. Glue strips of newspaper over the rock shapes to make them smooth.

4. Paint your model rock pool. Let it dry then cover it with PVA glue so it lasts longer.

5. Add seaweed made from wool and strips of green crepe paper.

6. Put your finds around your rock pool.

Useful words

artificial: Describes a thing made by people, not naturally.

cliff: A very steep and high rock form.

dunes: Mounds of sand piled up by the wind. You find sand dunes by the sea or in deserts.

fossil: Marks left by ancient animals found in some rocks.

life cycle: The way an animal grows and changes through its life.

rock pool: A pool of water left among rocks when the tide goes out and covered again when the tide comes in.

roots: The parts of a plant that grow down into the soil, holding it in place and taking up water.

scavenge: To look for scraps of food that have been left behind by people or other animals.

shoal: A group of fish.

tentacles: The long, bendy feelers of certain animals.

tide: The way the level of the sea rises and falls. There are two high tides and low tides each day.

29

About this book

This book encourages children to explore and discover science in the familiar environment of the seashore. By starting from 'where they are', it aims to increase children's knowledge and understanding of the world around them, encouraging them to examine objects and living things closely and from a more scientific perspective.

The habitat of the seashore is explored, focusing on the variety of life and how it has adapted. Questions are asked to build on children's natural curiosity and encourage them to think about what they are reading. Some questions send children back to the book to find the answers, others point to new ideas that, through discussion, the readers may 'discover' for themselves.

Index